Leadership Lessons From Intelligence

By Dr. Derrick L Randolph Sr.

Leadership Lessons from the Intelligence Community

Useful for the Kingdom of God

Supported by Biblical Principles

Copyrighted Material

DEDICATION

I dedicate Leadership Lessons to my family, friends, community and church family in Baltimore, Maryland.

Enjoy the Journey!

Preface

I'm writing to reach a community of leaders, who can relate to the intelligence community and information assurance principles and who can receive the guidance of scripture. For that small group of leaders, this leadership guide will be a treat.

Keep leading, keep managing and keep serving.

Be encouraged.

Table of Contents

We are always at war

One of the most difficult lessons for leaders to learn is that we are always at war. In industry, your competitor is looking for the advantage against you. In nation-state dominance, entire nations are seeking to gain the competitive advantage. China has publicly admitted to having hundreds of thousands of their own citizens, staffed for cyber war, during this age of information warfare. Athletes are growing taller and leaner, yet, stronger, faster, every year. Yesterday's centers are merely shooting guards in today's basketball games. Running backs are 250 pounds of muscle. I would run if I were a safety having to tackle a runaway running back in open field.

Everyone in business has been brought into the battlefield. Every piece of information is a source of intelligence. Every private conversation can be useful for gaining an edge.

As a Christian, I have to remind myself everyday that when I wake up, that I too have been drafted into war. Even as a citizen, and a responsible family man, I am trying to hold on to the money in my pocket. I am reminded that every commercial on the television screen is an aggressive and manipulative attempt to take what is rightfully mine.

Lesson #1 - *Be alert*

We have assets and we are at war to protect them.

Read 1 Peter chapter 5, verse 8.

The apostle Peter writes, "Be alert and of sober mind. Your enemy the devil prowls around like a roaring lion looking for someone to devour."

Since we are being targeted, we must always be alert, prepared, and able to operate both offensively, gaining the advantage, and defensively, sober enough to be on guard and to stop the roaring lions from having us for lunch.

Leaders, be on the lookout for attacks against your assets, the people, integrity, culture, systems, processes, data, reputation, and relationships that you hold dearly. Enjoy the fruit of your labor and success but continue to remain vigilant.

Lesson #2 - Stay awake

In Mark 13:33-36, Jesus advised his disciples to "Be on guard! Be alert! You do not know when that time will come. [34] It's like a man going away: He leaves his house and puts his servants in charge, each with their assigned task, and tells the one at the door to keep watch. "Therefore keep watch because you do not know when the owner of the house will come back—whether in the evening, or at midnight, or when the rooster crows, or at dawn. If he comes suddenly, do not let him find you sleeping."

Each of us is responsible for something. You are a leader in charge of something. Do not be caught sleeping on the job. I remember supervising a young man, who was blessed to have been hired, but on the first day of the job, he was lying back in his chair, watching television, and he was almost sleep. I asked him to turn the TV channel off, and to get a less comfortable chair. I thought he would be fired before the week was out, but he managed a successful career with us.

We need to stay awake and know what's going on:

Know what your people are doing:

- Know what their job is, and what peek performance looks like for their job role.
- Know what #s they will hit, products they will produce, and what larger product or service they are contributing to, so you can tell, which group or person is not hitting the mark.
- Know what is causing the delays, what barriers can be removed, sometimes the boulders are physical, financial, emotional, relational, etc. You have to ask, to find out.

Watch your systems:

Notice what output they are producing, e.g. bad data, good data, bad products, excellence?

Walk through everything, with everyone and see if every group, every input, output, handoff, and touchpoint is operating succinctly. If not, it's the leader's job to correct it. The staff will never find the time to make it a priority. The leader is assigned to be the "fixer".

Watch your data:

- All of your data tells a story.
- What are your numbers saying?
- Do you see a consistent patter? Of good? Or bad?
- Do the numbers make sense? If not, they don't lie. They are telling you something. Listen to the numbers tell their story.

Lesson #3 - People need to have a need to know

Everyone doesn't need to know what you know.

They need a need to know what you know!

In the Intelligence world, we have a principle of protecting information, an information assurance, that people should have a need to know what you know, if you are going to share it.

Leadership Lesson:

Be careful of what you share. If you tell it all to everyone you become the liability that puts yourself and others at risk. You can lose control of your organization when the wrong information gets loose. As certain levels, you are able to handle certain information, but everyone does not have the level of risk tolerance as you. Entire companies, organizations, and teams can falter because of your misstep. Remember that folks with a need to know, will know how to protect information, but folks that lack the need to know, will also lack the sensitivity required to protect it. Simply put, they will continue to let it fly in the wrong directions. People have a sense of obligation to share publicly what you tell them.

In the bible, Jesus tells the disciples that things said in secret will be shouted from the rooftops. Read Matthew 10:27, He advises them how to preach, proclaim and shout publicly the divine secrets that He has received from the father, in heaven. He tells them, "What I tell you in the dark, speak in the daylight; what is whispered in your ear, proclaim from the roofs. As a preacher myself, I welcome this command to proclaim the good news publicly; however, some details are private and are not meant to fall into the wrong hands. When you are the recipient of private information, only share public info public, and keep private information private. I have grown to a point where I hold those in high esteem who can hold their tongues and withhold the grandeur of knowing it all.

In fact, read Matthew 13:10-12. You will see that people will share even more information with you, that you need to know, if you will simply protect what you already know and share it only with those who need to know it.

The disciples came to him and asked, "Why do you speak to the people in parables?" [11] He replied, "Because the knowledge of the secrets of the kingdom of heaven has been given to you, but not to them. [12] Whoever has will be given more, and they will have an abundance. Whoever does not have, even what they have will be taken from them.

Lesson #4 - When they say don't tell it, don't...

When they say don't tell anyone, don't tell anyone

Bruh - don't tell anyone

Leadership Lesson: Keep private information private

I remember when my supervisor shared some information with me and told me not to share it with anyone. I left that private conversation to enter a team meeting. I shared that information with 2-3 persons. I knew I should not have let it slip, and it was confidential information. No way I should have been that careless. I asked them not to share it. Nevertheless, 15 minutes after my meeting ended, one of the team members went back to my supervisor to discuss that piece of discrete information. They even quoted me. They name dropped to my boss. I could not deny it or hide it. I admit I showed off what I knew and I got exposed. Lesson learned. I will never, ever fall for that 1 again. When they say don't share it. Don't share it!

Lesson #5 - Bring them along slowly.

There is a right time to tell it, not a minute sooner.

Read John 16:1-15. Here is another example of holding information, from Jesus. Jesus tells the disciples that I am going away and he is preparing them to take on the role of leadership on their own. Jesus is the son of God. He has spent considerable prayer, and alone time with the father, who is in heaven. Jesus has received a lot in prayer and He has withheld a lot of secrets from the disciples, but now it is time for them to learn the next level of secrets. Information that will help them as the new leaders of the church. Jesus was a good steward of the information that He received from the father. He did not tell the things He was not supposed to share. And He did not share them until the appropriate time. What wonderful lessons for us to learn from the master.

Jesus says, "All this I have told you so that you will not fall away. [2] They will put you out of the synagogue; in fact, the time is coming when anyone who kills you will think they are offering a service to God. [3] They will do such things because they have not known the Father or me. [4] I have told you this, so that when their time comes you will remember that I warned you about them. I did not tell you this from the beginning because I was with you, [5] but now I am going [away]…[12] "I have much more to say to you, more than you can now bear.

19

Lesson #6 – It's never your stuff

Don't take it personal, it's not yours

One of the hardest lessons is, it's not your stuff. Don't take it personal.

As a parent, I've learned to take the perspective that these are children of God, given to me to love and steward. In the end, they will grow up to be God's men and women. I will hopefully die in old age, leaving them behind to lead and raise their own families into adulthood. Knowing this, allows me to take my hands off them just a little, simply because God's got them.

I've learned the same in my vocation and ministry. One mentor advised us to take the same approach as he has. God this is your church not mine. You fix it. I've said that prayer as well.

But even in my vocation, I've learned to get fully engaged, 100%, give it my all, and build up everyone and everything in my path, to pursue excellence. I have also learned to stop my emotional investment at a certain place. I draw the line somewhere, because there are simply too many things that I cannot change.

I've learned that the people, the teams, the budget, are not really mine. I am the steward, for a season, but it's not my stuff. It's never your stuff, whether it is the mission, the ministry, the position. It's not yours. It always God's possessions. He will move new leaders into place and let the old ones go somewhere and start over again. He will scrap a mission and start a new one. Heck, if He is the potter and you are the clay, as He told the prophet Jeremiah, then He can scrap you and build a new you, so don't get too hooked on anything. Don't think anything is yours and yours alone. Even the bright ideas in our heads are not ours alone. I still believe that every time God gives me an idea for a message, a book, a business, etc. He is also giving it to so many others.

These ideas are like rain drops that fall and we either catch them or not. My mother used to say that there is nothing new under the sun. I believe may of us will get the same bright idea from God and only few of us will act on it. Nevertheless, these things are not ours.

Lesson – learn to take a step back, regather yourself and your composure and re-engage in the right mind. You are a servant, a steward of what God sets before you. Keep your head as you manage it.

Lesson #7 – Manage it well

Manage other people's stuff like you would your own

Speaking of managing someone else's stuff (from lesson #6), there's a biblical principle that says, learn to manage someone else's and He'll give you your own to manage.

Read Luke 16:1-12 when you can, about the Shrewd Manager. It is one of my favorite stories int eh bible, It's difficult to grasp the core principle of it. There are so many points being made in this story, but the big point hits in the end in verse 10-12, where Jesus concludes: Whoever can be trusted with very little can also be trusted with much, and whoever is dishonest with very little will also be dishonest with much. [11] So if you have not been trustworthy in handling worldly wealth, who will trust you with true riches? [12] And if you have not been trustworthy with someone else's property, who will give you property of your own? Just think Jesus was teaching this connection between managing your earthly wealth with being given spiritual wealth, but explains it in a parable, a story about a man who was managing money for someone and was about to get fired because he had not collected the money that was owed to his master. So he made side deals with everyone that owed money to at least get something from them, and in return maybe these customers would give him a place to live when he gets fired and kicked out.

He was certainly shrewd. He showed that he knew how to manage his master's business. He was dishonest but shrewd. This is a hard one but the principle is this. If you can manage someone else's stuff, well, then you will get the opportunity to manage your own. If you can manage your earthly life, then you will get a chance to manage a heavenly one as well.

This man managed the customer's past due balance for them, to get them off the hook. He managed his master's bottom line, by at least getting him some of the money and he managed to get a future place to stay in the process. He was shrewd.

I've learned that by going all in and giving my all managing someone else's mission, I brought more skill, tact, sense, and excellence into my own life. I am bothered when I see people unwilling to give their best on the job. I especially hate to see leaders unwilling to be challenged, stretched, and moved out of the place of complacency and into a place of expanded growth. This bothers me mainly because as a leader, you must grow in order for those within your realm of influence to grow. You have other leaders, superiors, peers, and direct reports that need to grow as well and they will only see it, when they see it in you. So, manage someone else's stuff well, and grow in the process.

Lesson #8 – Promotion comes from the Lord

When I look back, I've had many high moments when I was picked for something great, given a divine assignment or landed in a dream job. On the other hand, I've had many low moments when I consider my salary for those assignments.

I remember my first job like it was yesterday. I was working for $2 per hour as a teenager, in a seafood restaurant, in Park Heights, in Baltimore. I started in one location working with a friend for a friend of his family. Then I moved to a new location, in downtown Baltimore, on Fayette Street, running that small restaurant all alone. That was a rough start and it is a long story for me to explain why I had to start so low. I'll save it for another book. Nevertheless, I learned how to sell in that job. That launched me into selling and delivering newspapers, working a concession stand at Memorial Stadium, etc.

Flash forward, I'm out of college, degree in hand with Cum Laude honors and my first job was a part-time telemarking job, making minimum wage that was 3.25 per hour. That was a rough middle after a rough start. I learned to handle rejection on that job. One thing for sure is that I am not afraid to be told no.

Nevertheless, somehow I made it into the intelligence community. Hired from the commercial industry to a federal contractor and finally into a federal government agency. I was hired and was quickly moved into a position where I was in charge of it all (at least my small corner).

I worked tirelessly my first few years and thought I would get promoted for it. I learned quickly that it was all about relationships. In fact, the whole of life, in all areas and domains, everything is relational. Just think, we were created by a God that is relational. He showed up in our world in and as 3 different persons. He was the father who created us. The son, Jesus Christ, who redeemed us, and the Holy Spirit, who fills our hearts and comforts us and in 1 moment in history, He showed up as all 3 persons in the same place, each affirming the other. He was showing us the way to follow.

God is relational and so are we, but we forget it, when we go to work and try to accomplish our daily checklists and to-do lists of chores.

In my first conversation with a manager that wanted to help me get promoted, I was told to stick with them and they would help me. It felt like a back-room conversation where I was being introduced to the mob. It almost scared me a little. But I soon understood that I did not know all of the work required of me at that level. I did not fully operate at the next level, just yet and I did not have the capacity to manage my end of the relationship with the leaders above me. I did not take long for me to realize that I worked extraordinarily hard but I was not as deserving for the promotion as I thought I was. In fact, when I finally got that promotion that I was looking for, I was actually grateful for it and not feeling entitled to it.

I've since learned that "Promotion comes from the Lord". God chooses the appointed time. That's found in Psalm 75. Verses 6 & 7 read, "No one from the east or the west or from the desert can exalt themselves. It is God who judges: He brings one down, he exalts another.

God decides when it is the right time (for you), and He decides if you are the right person (for it). He moves each of us into position and places us in seats of authority for a season. We manage the mission for Him, and we ultimately know that God is judge.

Lesson #9 - Protect your heart (CIA)

One of the reasons I am writing this guide is because of this lesson here. As an information system security professional, I sat in my study reading the tenets of information security, realizing that so much of the computer world is like that of the spirit and of good leadership. We all have something to protect, good sense to guard and decisions that require good judgment.

Here's one parallel. We've learned to protect the (Confidentiality, integrity, availability) of your data.

I've similarly learned to protect the CIA of your heart.

C - Confidentiality – Protect your desire for doing good

I - integrity – Maintain your purity of heart

A - availability – Be available to people

These are strong commitments that will propel us in our leadership capacity. You know the song, saying and movie, that there's is a thin line between love & hate. I know there's a thin line between a corrupt heart, that becomes overbearing and abusive, and having a loving heart, that has genuine compassion for the people you lead. To stay on the right side of the line, you have to protect your heart, using CIA. Read Proverbs 4:23 which says, above all else, guard your heart, for everything you do flows from it.

Point #10 – Defense in Depth

I am talking to leaders, and I realize that many of us live three dimensionally. You most likely have a job, a purpose and an assignment. You are sent on assignment somewhere, to do a 9-to-5 job, with a God given purpose to fulfill as you do it.

Again, an assignment where you are sent to, to do a job (the work you do) to fulfill your purpose (the reason why you are there).

And guess what, you are anointed for it, but you need protection to be successful. You need to guard your anointing. The intelligence world has taught us a simple but very effective way to protect ourselves. It is called, defense in depth. Use it to guard your anointing.

In the IT world we learned many ways of protecting the different entry points to an IT system. We learned to place guards on every door (virtual, physical, and procedural). We learned that if the enemy cannot get access one way, they will try another. As a leader, guard your anointing or it will be attacked and either destroyed, stolen or corrupted right under your nose.

In 1 John 2:20 and 27, the leader explains that you have an anointing and the anointing remains in you, but you must guard it. The easiest way to lose it is to forget it. How can I forget that I have a purpose to fulfill when I am sent on an assignment, with a job to do? One way is to fall into the daily traps of leadership. It's when you lose focus. It's when you fight with the staff, when you lust for promotion, thirst for immediate gratitude, public recognition, and when you quit on the job (while still working), when you lose the commitment for your assignment and when you lose sight of your purpose. So, protect all 3:

Protect the Assignment

- Make visual reminders that you are on assignment:
- E.g. I am sent from God, I was asked to go there by my mentor, I was sent for by the leader, I was invited to bring change, etc.

Protect the Purpose

- Spend time daily being reminded of your purpose,
- E.g. why you are there: I am there to make a difference, help people along the way, to do good, to lift the spirit, to restore the balance, etc.

Protect the Job

- Dedicate time to learn your job, e.g. spend 30 days doing research, spend a weekend with your job description, spend your month learning your mission, functions & performance goals.

May God bless you in your spiritual journey, your vocational pursuit and in your relationship building

Leadership is a Journey

Dr. Derrick L. Randolph, Sr.

Journey of Faith Ministries

www.ingramcontent.com/pod-product-compliance
Lightning Source LLC
Chambersburg PA
CBHW050453110426
42744CB00013B/1976